PERFECT PETS

Cats

Kathryn Hinds

BENCHMARK BOOKS

MARSHALL CAVENDISH

NEW YORK

Benchmark Books
Marshall Cavendish Corporation
99 White Plains Road
Tarrytown, New York 10591

© 1999 by Kathryn Hinds

Library of Congress Cataloging-in-Publication Data
Hinds, Kathryn, date.
Cats / Kathryn Hinds.
p.   cm. — (Perfect Pets)
Includes bibliographical references (p.   ).
Summary: Explores the lore, different breeds, characteristics,
and habits of these popular animals.
ISBN 0-7614-0794-4 (lib. bdg.)
1. Cats—Juvenile literature. [1. Cats.] I. Title. II. Series.
SF445.7.H55   1999   636.8—DC21   97-21757   CIP   AC

Photo research by Ellen and Matthew Dudley

Cover photo: *Animals Animals:* Robert Maier
Back cover photo: *Peter Arnold Inc:* BIOS/C. Ruoso

The photographs in this book are used by permission and
through the courtesy of: *Animals Animals:* Gerard Lacz, 1, 20,
30; Robert Pearcy, 15; Robert Maier, 16, 19; Phil Degginger, 17;
Fritz Prenzel Photo, 21; Reneé Stockdale, 24; Oxford Scientific
Films, 25; Carson Baldwin, Jr., 26; Norvia Behling, 28. *Art Re-
source:* Erich Lessing, Art Resource, NY, 4; The Pierpont
Morgan Library, Art Resource, NY, 9. *Corbis Bettmann:* Agence
France Presse/Corbis-Bettmann, 29. *Peter Arnold, Inc:* Gerard
Lacz, 6; BIOS (J-J Etienne), 8; James, L. Amos, 18. *Photo
Researchers, Inc.:* Rod Planck, 3; P.W. Grace, 7; E. Hanumantha
Rao, 10; Gregory G. Dimijian, 11; Peter B. Kaplan, 12; Mary
Eleanor Browning, 13 (top); Larry Voight, 13 (bottom); Jean-
Michel Labat/Jacana, 14; Dennis Purse, 22; Catherine Ursillo,
23; Renee Lynn, 27.

Printed in Hong Kong
6   5   4   3   2   1

To Owen,
in memory of Mowzer

With special thanks to The Cat Fanciers' Association, Inc.,
especially to Edna Field, for assisting the author's research

The ancient Egyptian goddess Bast was the divine protector of cats and often took the form of a cat herself, as in this bronze statue.

Cats

are among the most popular pets in North America. But in ancient Egypt they were more than just pets; they were the special animals of a great and powerful goddess. This goddess was called Bast. Statues showed her as a woman with a cat's head or as a beautiful cat wearing necklaces and gold earrings. Her main temple was home to hundreds of cats and kittens. Every year a festival was held there, and thousands of people came to sing, dance, and feast in her honor.

Bast was a goddess of love, joy, and motherhood. She also represented the gentle warmth of the sun, which made all things grow. Sometimes Bast's father, the sun god Ra, also became a cat. In this form he fought the serpent of darkness.

Stories from ancient Rome told how the cat was created by the moon goddess Diana. Her brother Apollo had just made the lion, and she wanted to tease him by making a smaller version of his creation. It is easy to see how the cat's round, glowing eyes reminded the Romans of the moon.

Europeans in the late Middle Ages thought of the cat as a creature of the night. But to many, night was a time of evil

A Persian cat perches in a tree, keeping watch over its territory below.

witchcraft. Cats went from being the companions of goddesses to the companions of witches. People even thought that witches could turn themselves into cats.

All over the world people have believed in the magical powers of cats. Indonesian farmers gave their cats baths to make rain fall on the rice fields. In Romania newlyweds rocked a cat in a cradle so that they would soon have a baby. Sailors in many countries thought that a cat's behavior could predict storms at sea. In France stories were told about cat

A cat can be fierce—and frightening—when it is angry or afraid.

The Black Cat's Luck

During the fourteenth through the sixteenth centuries, most Europeans thought that any strange cat might be a witch in disguise. One sort of cat was considered most evil of all: the black cat. **Superstitions** about black cats have been common ever since. In the 1800s many African Americans in the southern United States thought black cats could cause disease, death, and other miseries. Even today there are people in Europe and the United States who feel it is bad luck for a black cat to cross your path. But in parts of these same places there is also a traditional belief that it is good luck to have a black cat for a pet!

8

magicians. The most famous one was about Puss in Boots, in which the hero's talking cat helped him defeat an ogre and marry a princess.

People still enjoy reading and writing stories about magical cats. And people who live with cats know that their pets bring a very real kind of magic into their lives. In fact, all people with pets know this magic, because it is the magic of love.

"Puss in Boots" has been a favorite story since at least 1695, when Charles Perrault included it in one of Europe's first books of fairy tales.

The tiger is the largest member of the cat family. It lives in Asia.

Domestic

cats, or house cats, belong to the same animal family as lions and leopards. The members of the cat family live in almost every type of natural **habitat.** They range in size from the huge Siberian tiger to the little black-footed cat of southern Africa. But even with so much variety, all the members of the cat family behave in very similar ways.

The ancestor of the **domestic** cat was probably the African wildcat. This animal is a little larger than most modern house cats and has longer legs. It is slender and reddish colored, and it can be tamed quite easily.

The African wildcat probably started living near humans in the Middle East, about ten thousand years ago. This was the time when people first began farming—and storing the grain they grew. When mice came to

The African wildcat is a night-time hunter of rodents and other small animals.

11

eat the grain, wildcats came to eat the mice. People quickly realized how useful these mouse hunters were and tamed some of them. Within two thousand years these tame wild-cats evolved into domestic cats like those of today.

There are now more than forty different **breeds,** or types, of domestic cat. The oldest breed is the Egyptian mau, which appears in paintings from ancient Egypt. Another breed that originally came from North Africa is the Abyssinian. It looks like the cats in ancient Egyptian statues. With its sandy-red fur, it also resembles the African wildcat. It has a lively and affectionate personality.

Two of the most popular breeds are the Persian and the Siamese. The Persian has very long fur and a flat face. The Siamese has short fur in two colors: a light color on its body, and a darker one on its ears, tail, face, and legs. Another breed, the Himalayan, is a cross between these two breeds. It has the long fur of a Persian and the color pattern of a Siamese.

A blue Persian cat. (When describing fur colors, "blue" usually refers to various shades of gray.)

The earliest North American breed is the American shorthair. It is descended from the farm cats and house cats that accompanied European colonists in the seventeenth century. It is smart, strong, and lively. The Maine coon cat is another well-loved North American breed. It is very large and its fur is long and shaggy.

There are some cat breeds with rather unusual qualities. Rex cats have wavy or even curly fur. The Manx and Cymric cats have very short tails or no tails at all. The Japanese bobtail has a small tail that looks almost like that of a rabbit. The Scottish fold has ears that are naturally folded forward. The American curl has

The American shorthair (top) can be one of thirty-three different colors or color combinations.

The Scottish fold (bottom) is a quiet, affectionate breed that began on a Scottish farm in the 1960s.

13

ears that curl backward at their tips. But the most unusual breed of all must be the Sphynx. This cat has very large ears—and no fur at all! Although it may look strange, it makes a good pet for cat lovers with allergies.

There are many other breeds of cats. Most domestic cats, however, do not belong to any particular breed, or they are a mix of several breeds. Animal shelters have many lovable **mixed-breed** cats waiting for just the right person to adopt them.

The Japanese bobtail appears in ancient Japanese sculptures and paintings. It is a traditional belief in Japan that this cat brings good luck to the household.

A Cat Show

Some people like to take their cats to cat shows, where they can win ribbons and recognition. Most of the cats competing in a cat show belong to specific breeds. A cat competes against other cats of the same breed and of the same color within the breed. Highly trained judges examine each cat to see how well it meets certain standards. At some cat shows there is also a household pet competition, which mixed-breed cats can enter. In this competition the judges give prizes based on the cats' personalities, unique qualities, and looks. For many people the highlight of a cat show comes when the judges present the award for the best cat in the show. But it is fun to go just to see and learn about the many different kinds of cats that the show brings together.

This kitten and dwarf rabbit have an unusual relationship—most cats would rather chase a rabbit than make friends with it.

There

is nothing quite as comforting as having a cat beside you, purring and letting you stroke its soft fur. Pet cats can be wonderfully affectionate. Most of the time they enjoy, and often crave, human company. At other times they may act as if they're not the least bit interested in the people around them. This makes them seem distant, but also mysterious.

The cat is not like most of the other domestic animals, which have all been bred to serve humans in some way. The cat's only obvious usefulness is in catching mice and rats. This is its natural behavior, not something people trained it to do—and not something it can be commanded to do. Cats are famous for doing things only if they feel like it. This independence is one of the qualities many people like about cats.

Another thing that makes the cat such a special pet is that it brings a touch of wild nature into our homes and lives. This is because the domestic cat has changed very little from its wild ancestor. A house cat dozing on the sofa can instantly

A cat seldom lets a fence get in its way—with its natural athletic skills, it simply jumps or climbs to the top of the fence and then uses it for a walkway!

turn into a deadly hunter if it senses a mouse or any other small animal nearby. In fact, the domestic cat has been called one of nature's most perfect hunters.

To help them hunt, cats have very keen senses of hearing and vision. They hear much better than humans or dogs. They can move their ears around to catch the tiniest sounds made by their **prey.** They can see the slightest movements out of the corners of their eyes. Cats often hunt at night, and in low light they see up to ten times better than people do. Cats also have a better sense of smell than we do. They use this sense mainly to get information about other cats. Whiskers give them information about prey that they have captured and also help with their sense of balance.

Cats' bodies are designed to be graceful, flexible, and agile. They are strong and muscular. A cat can jump higher than you can stretch—even on your tiptoes! It can walk along a very narrow rail or ledge without losing its balance. Over a short distance a cat can run faster than a dog the same size. All these abilities are part of the cat's great hunting and survival skills.

Cats have a lot of stored-up energy. When hunting doesn't use up this energy, cats release it in other ways. They race around the house or chase their tails. Or they play—sometimes with small animals that they have caught. Cats really seem to enjoy playing, and it helps them practice their hunting skills.

Much of a cat's hunting behavior comes from instinct, but a lot of it must be learned as a

This cat is playing with a mouse it has caught.

kitten. Mother cats are very caring and protective, and they are patient teachers. They show their kittens how to hunt. If a kitten is too young when it is separated from its mother, it may be able to catch prey, but it might never know what to do with it.

Usually the only time a cat naturally lives with other cats is when it is a kitten. Except for lions, members of the cat family live alone most of the time. All types of cats are very territorial. This means that a cat claims a certain area as its own. The cat patrols this area often and defends it whenever necessary. That is why a cat will

How Cats Always Land on Their Feet

Throughout history people have been amazed by the cat's ability to fall from a great height and still land, unharmed, on its feet. This is possible because of the cat's incredibly flexible body. Even if a cat is upside down when it falls, it can contract its muscles to turn its head and forelegs so that they face the ground. At the same time it rotates its hind legs to bring them into line with the front half of the body. Then the cat arches its back and stretches its legs down to meet the ground. And all this takes only one-eighth of a second!

These kittens are full of energy and eager to explore their world—but they seem to have worn their mother out!

fight with strange cats that come into its yard. When more than one cat live in the same house, they often divide the house into territories. If each cat stays in its own area, they should get along fairly well.

Cats have many ways of communicating with other cats and with humans. They purr when they are content, or sometimes when they are nervous and need to comfort themselves. They hiss and growl when they are angry or frightened. When they are upset, they may yowl. They meow in many different ways—there are meows that mean "Hello," "I'm hungry," "Please pet me," and more.

Cats also communicate through body language. A frightened or angry cat arches its back, makes its fur stand on end, lashes its tail, and lays its ears back. A hunting cat crouches with all its muscles tensed and its tail twitching. A cat gives itself a thorough bath when it is feeling relaxed and content. When feeling insecure, a cat may wash just a paw or shoulder. An alert, happy cat trots along with its ears held slightly forward and its tail straight up. A cat will often come to greet its favorite people in this way.

Cats have very flexible bodies and almost always enjoy a good stretch.

When two friendly cats meet, they often rub noses. A cat may like to rub noses with its human friends, too.

23

A scratching post like this is wonderful for indoor cats—it gives them a place to perch, to play, to climb, and to sharpen their claws.

Cats

make good pets because they are beautiful, affectionate, and easy to care for. They can live mostly outdoors or mostly indoors. An outdoor cat needs a place to take shelter during bad weather. An indoor cat needs room to move about and at least one window it can look out of. It must also have a litter box to go to the bathroom in, which should be cleaned once a day.

All cats need a bowl of fresh water every day. They also need a cat food that gives them complete nutrition. Dry food and canned food are both fine, but some cats like one better than the other. Cat food companies also make several types of treats. A cat can have one or two of these a day for "dessert" or as a reward for good behavior.

Many cats enjoy drinking milk and eating table scraps. However, too much milk or

A little bit of milk can be a welcome treat.

human food can upset a cat's stomach. And a cat must never be given bones or it may choke.

Cats do most of their own grooming. They spend a great deal of time licking themselves clean. Just about the only time a cat needs to be given a bath is if it has a very bad case of fleas. Then a **veterinarian** might recommend washing its fur with a special flea-killing shampoo. Cats with long fur need to be brushed every day. Short-furred cats only need to be brushed now and then.

This cat seems to enjoy soaking in a tub, but most cats are not so calm about getting a bath.

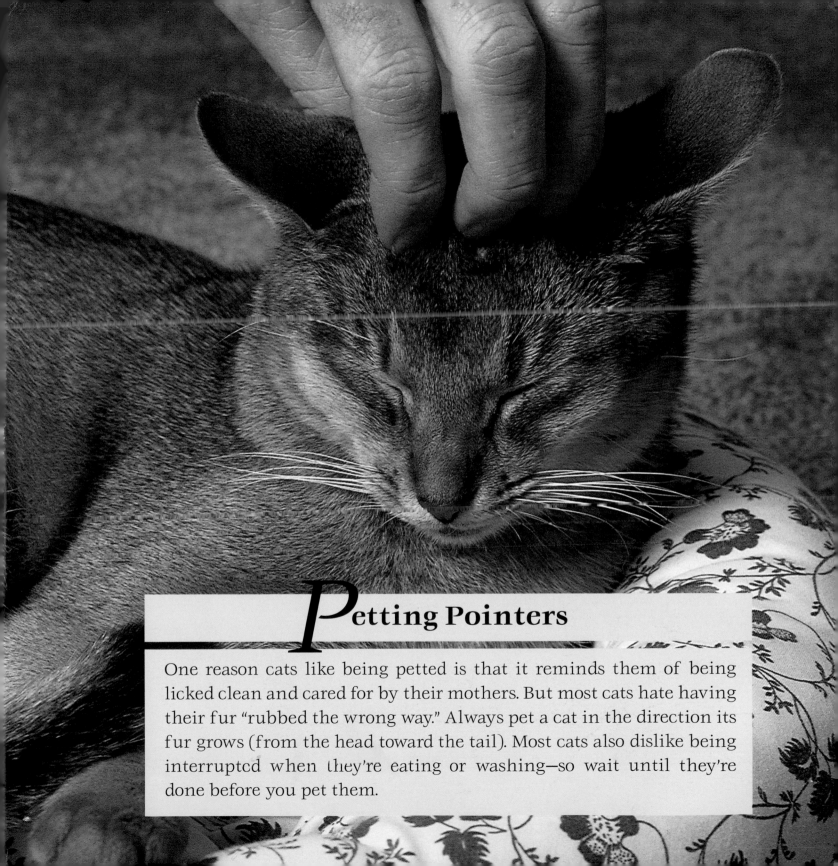

Petting Pointers

One reason cats like being petted is that it reminds them of being licked clean and cared for by their mothers. But most cats hate having their fur "rubbed the wrong way." Always pet a cat in the direction its fur grows (from the head toward the tail). Most cats also dislike being interrupted when they're eating or washing—so wait until they're done before you pet them.

Once a year every pet cat should visit the veterinarian for a complete checkup. At this time the cat should also get shots to protect it from **rabies** and other serious diseases. And if a cat is sick, injured, or behaving strangely, it is always a good idea to call the veterinarian for advice.

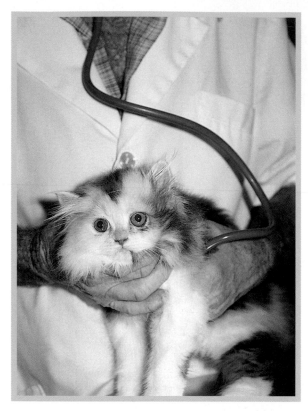

This kitten may look uncomfortable, but regular checkups will help it live a healthy and happy life.

Clean and safe shelter, healthy food, fresh water, medical care—these are the basics that a cat should have. And if you want a cat to be the best possible pet, there is one more thing that it needs: your love. Be sure to spend time with your cat every day. Pet it or scratch it behind the ears. Play with it—cats love to bat at a dangling string or chase a bouncy little ball. But also respect your cat's wishes if it wants to be left alone. Don't be too loud or rowdy near your cat. A cat is much happier around people when it is treated gently.

When you care for a cat, you will be part of a very special relationship. One young cat lover calls his pet "your average everyday furry friend." Like millions of others, he has found that cats are beautiful and interesting companions who ask little and give a great deal of love in return.

A Cat in the White House

One of the world's most famous cats is Socks, the pet of the First Family of the United States. Socks began life as a stray, living in the bushes near the home of Chelsea Clinton's piano teacher in Little Rock, Arkansas. On March 29, 1990, Chelsea saw the black-and-white kitten and fell in love with him. The Clintons adopted him and took him home to the governor's mansion. When Bill Clinton became president in 1993, Socks moved to the White House with the rest of the family. Socks has his own Secret Service agent to hold his leash and take him on walks through the White House. In the winter Socks likes to spend time in the furnace room in the basement, and in the summer he enjoys stretching out on a cool marble floor. But his favorite place of all is Chelsea's room.

Fun Facts

🐾 There are roughly 64 million pet cats in North America today.

🐾 Americans spend more money on cat food than on baby food.

🐾 The average mother cat can give birth to up to eight kittens at a time.

🐾 Kittens are born blind. All kittens' eyes are blue when they first open (about two weeks after birth). The eyes get their permanent color later.

🐾 A grown-up female cat is called a queen. A male cat is called a tom.

🐾 Well-cared-for, healthy cats live for about twelve years. The oldest cat on record was twenty-seven years old when it died.

🐾 The first cat show was held in London, in 1871.

🐾 Some famous cat lovers: Confucius, Muhammad, Mark Twain, Florence Nightingale, Theodore Roosevelt, Pablo Picasso, Queen Victoria, and Jay Leno.

Glossary

breed: A group of animals that are descended from common ancestors and share the same basic characteristics, including the way they look.

domestic: Describes a type of animal that has been tamed and trained to live among humans and help them.

habitat: The area or kind of environment in which an animal normally lives.

mixed-breed: An animal that does not belong to any particular breed and may be a mix of several breeds.

prey: An animal that is hunted by another animal for food.

rabies: A deadly disease that can affect warm-blooded animals. An animal usually catches rabies from the bite of a creature that already has the disease.

superstition: A traditional belief that has no sensible reason behind it.

veterinarian: A doctor who takes care of animals.

Find Out More About Cats

Alderton, David. *The Eyewitness Handbook of Cats.* New York: Dorling Kindersley, 1992.

Clutton-Brock, Juliet. *Cat.* New York: Knopf, 1991.

Edney, Andrew, and David Taylor. *101 Essential Tips: Cat Care.* New York: Dorling Kindersley, 1992.

Evans, Mark. *ASPCA Pet Care Guide for Kids: Kitten.* New York: Dorling Kindersley, 1992.

Multimedia Cats. Inroads Interactive. (CD-ROM)

Virtual Reality: Cat. Dorling Kindersley Multimedia. (CD-ROM)

About the Author

Kathryn Hinds was given her first kitten when she was three years old. She has been a cat lover ever since. She grew up near Rochester, New York, and always wanted to be a writer. Now she lives in Georgia's Blue Ridge Mountains with her husband, their son, a cat, and a dog. Her books for children include a book about pet rabbits and books about the Romans, the Vikings, and other cultures of the past.